YELLOWSTONE ON FIRE!

BY THE STAFF OF THE BILLINGS GAZETTE

Revised edition. Story by Robert Ekey and Pat Bellinghausen
Photos by Larry Mayer, Bob Zellar, James Woodcock and Judy Tell

Billings Gazette
The Source.

The staff of *The Billings Gazette*

Story by Robert Ekey and Pat Bellinghausen

Photos by Larry Mayer, Bob Zellar, James Woodcock, and Judy Tell

Graphics by John Potter

Published by The Billings Gazette.

Library of Congress Catalog Card Number 94-078562

ISBN 0-9627618-7-7

Printed in U.S.A.

For copies of this book contact:

The Billings Gazette
P.O. Box 36300
Billings, MT 59107-6300
Call toll free 1-800-927-2345
In Billings, call 657-1200

Front cover: A firestorm moves toward the Norris Geyser Basin on Aug. 20, 1988.
LARRY MAYER

First page: Old Faithful geyser, the most famous tourist attraction in Yellowstone Park, erupts against a smoke-filled sky.
BOB ZELLAR

Title page: The North Fork Fire illuminates the night skyline south of West Yellowstone.
LARRY MAYER

Back cover: Stephen Albers, a sawyer on the Clover-Mist Fire, stands silhouetted against the glowing flames.
JAMES WOODCOCK

ACKNOWLEDGMENTS

Covering the daily events of Yellowstone National Park has been a major focus of *The Billings Gazette* for years, and it remains so even today. But for more than three months in the summer of 1988, the staff of *The Gazette* fought an unparalleled race against deadlines, distance and nature to bring news of the Yellowstone Park fires to its readers. This book captures the essence of those journalistic efforts and helps explain the effects of the devastating blazes and the park policies that came into play.

Yellowstone Park, at its nearest point, is more than 100 miles from Billings, yet photographers and reporters made the journey day in and day out for months on end, shuttling film and stories to editors and the awaiting presses. On some days, *The Gazette* had as many as 12 reporters, photographers and editors in or around the park, covering the fires with an intensity matched only by the blazes themselves.

Special recognition must be given to reporter Pat Bellinghausen and photographer Bob Zellar, the first journalists to break the news of the park fires to the world. They helped trigger the largest reporting effort ever undertaken by *The Billings Gazette,* which was named a Pulitzer Prize finalist for its work.

Special thanks also must go reporter Vikki McLaughlin, who wrote fire stories each day for months; reporter Tom Howard who rarely missed a day on the fire lines; former *Gazette* reporter Robert Ekcy who covered the fires and who wrote the first edition of *Yellowstone On Fire!;* and virtually every other reporter and editor who worked in the park covering the fires, or editing the massive volume of stories from their desks at *The Gazette.*

This undertaking could never have been successful without the efforts of *Gazette* Chief Photographer Larry Mayer who flew his own airplane on 20 round-trips to the park to shoot aerial photos. He and his photo team of Bob Zellar, James Woodcock and former *Gazette* photographer Judy Tell provided the award-winning photography for this book.

Richard J. Wesnick
Editor of *The Billings Gazette*

Above: Days after fire swept along the Madison River, elk return to graze. Wildlife often were seen in recently burned areas seeking mineral-rich ash. BOB ZELLAR

Next page: Flames jump above the treetops as a firestorm sweeps north of the town of Silver Gate. JAMES WOODCOCK

CONTENTS

Early morning smoke blankets the fire camp at Grant Village as firefighters start their day. BOB ZELLAR

INTRODUCTION

Drought, lightning and unrelenting wind joined forces in Yellowstone forests in 1988. From July through September, nature replayed an ancient drama in the Yellowstone high country.

Huge fires have been part of life in Yellowstone since glaciers retreated 12,000 years ago, but the fires of 1988 were the largest in more than 100 years.

Some of the dozen major 1988 fires started in national forests outside Yellowstone Park. Most of the burned land in the 12 million acre Greater Yellowstone Area was in the 2.2 million acre park. When the fires were out, a study using aerial photography indicated that 1.4 million acres had burned, including 988,925 acres in Yellowstone Park.

A year later, a more detailed National Park Service study incorporating satellite images of the park indicated that the actual acreage inside the park was less: 793,880 acres burned or 36 percent of all park land.

The fires defied the experts, burning beyond analysts' worst-case forecasts and beyond the control of the nation's best firefighters.

An army of thousands of firefighters from all over the Western United States and as far away as Florida and Hawaii mobilized to fight the Yellowstone area fires. At the height of the battle, the U.S. Army and later the Marine Corps sent troops to the fire lines. It was the largest forest firefighting effort ever.

Firefighters built more than 800 miles of fire line and airplanes dropped more than a million gallons of fire retardant, but they couldn't stop the fires.

The giant fires advanced 5 to 10 miles a day. One fire traveled 14 miles in three hours. Smoke billowed 10 miles into the air, shrouding the park in a thick, acrid cloud.

Fires forced road closures and evacuations that cut heavily into tourism at peak summer season in 1988.

Left: A profusion of wildflowers surrounds new lodgepole pines and burned tree trunks near Madison Junction.

BOB ZELLAR

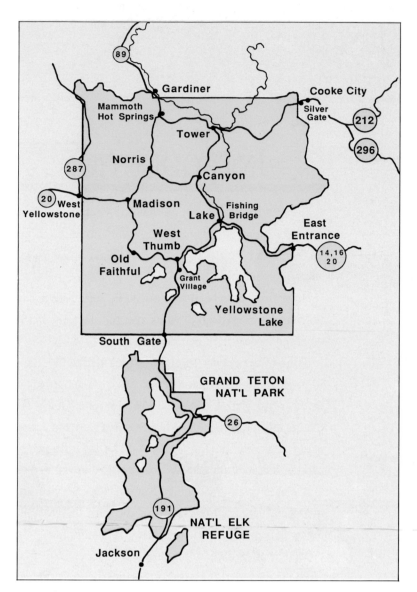

*Forest fires swept across 40 percent of Yellowstone National Park during
the summer of 1988, threatening many developments in the park and
communities along its boundaries.* MAP BY JOHN POTTER

Some firefighting decisions turned the heat on federal land managers as people in park border towns feared for their property and the American public saw television reports and headlines about fires sweeping Yellowstone, the beloved first national park. Some of the lightning-caused fires that started in the park and in the wilderness outside initially were not fought because of natural burn policies. Firefighters were not ordered to suppress some early summer blazes till late July.

In the end, it was fall rain and snow that cooled the fires. As the smoke cleared, a mosaic of black, brown and green was seen in the forests. The fires left green trees untouched amid stands of charred tree trunks.

Much of the burned land is in Yellowstone's back country, out of sight of visitors who travel only by car. Still, motorists will see the fires' effects on a drive from the south entrance to Grant Village, or from Old Faithful to West Yellowstone or Madison. The forest was destroyed or renewed, depending on the viewer's perspective.

A spectacular wildflower show played in spring and summer of 1989. Delicate, yellow glacier lilies dotted the black, sooty soil along river banks as soon as snow melted. Later in the summer, visitors in the Tower Junction area waded waist-deep in pink-purple fireweed covering hills as far as the eye could see.

Many tourists took in the new views. The park's visitor count increased after the fire year, hitting a record 3 million in 1992 and approaching that mark in 1993.

Tourists who stooped to look found inch-tall lodge-pole pines sprouting where ancient trees had burned. The centuries old trees had left behind seeds in pine cones that would only open in the heat of a fire.

Each plant and animal species showed its adaptability to fire.

Scientists flocked to the park to study the complex natural changes the huge fires triggered.

"Yellowstone has not lost its ability to teach us and inspire us," Robert Barbee, park superintendent during the fires, told a scientific conference years later. "We survived the most amazing event of our lives. It was an awesome lesson in nature's power and human frailty."

Firefighters scramble to protect buildings at Old Faithful when a firestorm rages over them. BOB ZELLAR

THE SIEGE OF 1988

As fire raged through Yellowstone National Park's lodge-pole pines on the edge of Grant Village, experienced firefighters stared wide-eyed at the spectacle as they prepared to make their last stand. All nonessential personnel from their nearby fire camp huddled along the shores of Yellowstone Lake, the designated "safe" spot—safe because it was open and people could wade into the frigid waters if necessary to avoid the fire.

By that Monday afternoon in July, the blaze already had overrun all efforts to stop it and the firefighters, poised with their hoses at the edge of the forest, were the village's last defense. Brush had been removed from around buildings that make up the new $15 million development in the southern end of Yellowstone. Firefighters stood ready to knock the fire out of the trees before it could roar into the hotels, restaurants and shops and their camp.

As the fire approached, hoses went off like cannons aimed at the sky. The firefighters were successful and, within two hours, the fire camp's caterer was serving dinner.

It was a dramatic scene in Yellowstone at the time; something that had never occurred before. But that was early in the 1988 fire season and the sight of firefighters working feverishly to save towns would be repeated dozens of times in August and September, until fall snows doused the fires.

By the time the historic fire season ended, aerial photos showed that fires scorched nearly 1.4 million acres of Yellowstone National Park and adjacent national forests. The flames swept across the drought-ridden region despite a $140 million effort which, at its peak, included 9,500 firefighters, 117 aircraft and more than 100 fire engines from

Firefighter Jill Jayne stares at the flames of the Red Fire burning near Lewis Lake in southern Yellowstone.
BOB ZELLAR

throughout the country. Two people died and hundreds more suffered minor injuries and fire-related illness.

Yellowstone's fire problems started early in the summer. On June 23, a lone bolt of lightning touched off the Shoshone Fire, the first of the season, in the southern end of the park. Two days later, the Fan Fire was spotted in the northwestern corner of the park and, within a week, the Red Fire started near the Shoshone.

Park rangers watched Yellowstone's fires early in the summer, but allowed them to burn under what became known as the "let it burn" policy. During 15 years under that policy—which allows natural wildfires to burn as long as they do not threaten life or property—only 34,000 acres had burned in the park.

The Shoshone Fire burned 160 acres during its first 30 days. During the second week of July, the total area of burned land in the park doubled to 17,000 acres. That week the Shoshone and Red fires burned toward each other. The Clover and Mist fires were burning in the eastern end of the park. The fire season was in full swing with a sudden increase in the size and numbers of fires.

On July 22, the Shoshone Fire exploded to 1,000 acres. By the end of the next day, it was 4,500 acres and on July 26 it roared to the edge of Grant Village.

July 22 also was a bad day outside Yellowstone.

Someone gathering firewood in the Targhee National Forest in Idaho accidentally started a fire within 200 yards of the park's western boundary. It quickly spread into the park and became the North Fork Fire, one of the most frustrating and damaging blazes of the season.

The extreme burning conditions—downed logs in the forest had less moisture than kiln-dried lumber—prompted park officials to adopt a policy of full suppression. All new fire starts would be aggressively attacked and firefighters would work to contain the fires already burning out of control.

Weather and landscape always are factors in forest

Above: Scores of fire crews respond to a call to help defend buildings at Grant Village. Throughout the summer, firefighters from across the nation helped protect park developments and nearby communities. LARRY MAYER

Right: An aerial view shows fire encroaching on Grant Village, one of the Yellowstone's largest developments catering to tourists. LARRY MAYER

fires. Ironically, Yellowstone's magnificent landscape contributed heavily to the intensity of fire during the summer of 1988. Deeply glaciated, high-elevation mountains give way to flat plateaus and broad valleys covered with dense lodgepole pine forests and crossed by few roads. The expanses of forest, devoid of prominent breaks or access, hampered firefighting efforts.

While the landscape played a role, weather was the critical difference in 1988. The region started drying out in the fall of 1987 when seasonal rains failed to materialize. A record-low snowpack and early spring runoff aggravated the situation to the point that even spring rain did not help. By mid-June, the Palmer Drought Index—which measures precipitation, soil moisture and evaporation—showed that the Yellowstone region was in the grips of extreme drought. When high-speed, warm winds joined the scene, it set the stage for the worst fire season in the park's history.

Yellowstone, designated the world's first national park in 1872, occupies 2.2 million acres of high country in northwestern Wyoming and southern Montana. But it is not an island of wild lands. It is surrounded by Grand Teton National Park and six national forests that share similar topography and wildlife to make up the Yellowstone ecosystem.

Fires in the Yellowstone area in 1988 crossed boundaries between national parks and forests as easily as elk on their winter migration. The U.S. Forest Service and the Park Service, which manage the land, worked together to coordinate the fire-suppression effort. Trained fire-management teams set up a command post in the small town of West Yellowstone to disburse firefighters, equipment and supplies and to coordinate the effort. Firefighting teams were composed mostly of experienced U.S. Forest Service workers.

As the fire encroached on Grant Village, guests and employees were asked to leave. But dozens of reporters flocked to the scene. Yellowstone is dear to the hearts of millions of people, and any activity there draws greater attention than a similar event elsewhere.

A few days after the Shoshone Fire swept to the edge of Grant Village, the North Fork Fire began a run toward Old Faithful. Although the fire was six miles away, firefighters were assigned to Old Faithful to protect the historic log inn and other buildings around the famous geyser. Even the distant threat of fire at Old Faithful drew more national attention than

actual flames at Grant Village. That attention shed considerable public light on the "let it burn" policy.

Interior Secretary Donald Hodel visited the park on July 27 and expressed support for Yellowstone's fire management policy. Before Hodel's visit, the fires in Yellowstone had burned fewer than 50,000 acres—less than 2 percent of the park. When Hodel returned to Yellowstone in September, on a fact-finding mission for President Ronald Reagan, fires in the greater Yellowstone area were approaching 1 million acres. He announced later that the fire management policy would get a thorough review.

When Hodel first visited the park, extensive firefighting efforts already were under way. Helicopters dropped burning Ping-Pong–size balls of fuel in the

Previous page:
Firefighter Clyde
Johnson watches as the
Red Fire approaches the
Lewis Lake campground.
BOB ZELLAR

Above: Flames leap up
tree trunks near Grant
Village, evidence of the
tinder-dry conditions in
the forested areas.
BOB ZELLAR

*Right: A helicopter dips
water from Crazy Creek to
drop on the Clover-Mist Fire
northeast of Yellowstone.
Dozens of helicopters
dropped 10 million gallons
of water on fires in the
greater Yellowstone area.*
BOB ZELLAR

forests in front of the North Fork Fire. The burning
balls started small fires, which were sucked toward
the larger blaze. This was designed to eradicate fuel
and leave the North Fork Fire nothing to burn.

But Yellowstone's 1988 fires frustrated such traditional firefighting techniques. In a phenomenon known
as "spotting," heavy winds lifted hot embers above
the treetops and deposited them beyond fire lines and
backfires, starting new fires.

Despite the extreme fire activity, most firefighters
and park officials remained optimistic that they could
stop the flames. One exception was Larry Caplinger,
incident commander of the North Fork Fire. As early
as July 27, he said, "We could be in for the beginning
of the Siege of 1988."

Firefighters employed some of the latest technology available to fight the fires. Infrared maps of the
park were made during high-altitude nighttime flights
and handed to fire commanders the next morning so
they could monitor fire progress and plot their strategy. Helicopters and air tankers dropped water and
flame retardant on the leading edges of the fires. But
firefighters also used some of the oldest techniques
available. Teams of pack horses and mules hauled supplies to "spike camps" in the Yellowstone back country where firefighters slept on the ground.

Early firefighting efforts were fruitless and the fires intensified daily. The unprecedented, persistent winds continued to fan the fires and aggravate the dry conditions. The fires started running almost a mile daily. Strategy changed from building containment lines in front of some fires to narrowing the fire front by pinching the flanks.

A team of fire-behavior experts arrived in West Yellowstone late in July to predict where the fires would burn by the end of August. While they were experienced in predicting fire growth in terms of days, this was the first attempt at predicting fire growth for an entire month.

The experts worked for two days studying historical weather patterns, fire behavior and the ages of the forests in the path of the fires. They fed the information into computers and, during the first days of August, presented their predictions to fire commanders and Park Service and Forest Service officials.

They used large maps of the fire perimeters with clear plastic overlays to predict where the fires would be on Aug. 15 and Aug. 31. But, even as they made their presentation to a meeting of officials at West Yellowstone on Aug. 2, the perimeters of some fires were burning past the Aug. 15 prediction lines.

The fires had made major runs while the prediction team was still feeding data into computers. The pro-

jections said the fires, which encompassed 125,000 acres, would grow by 25 to 50 percent in 30 days. Within five days, the fires had exceeded the acreage projections for the end of the month.

The Fan Fire in the northwestern corner of the park was making a mad dash toward the northern park boundary, threatening to spill over onto private lands owned by the Church Universal and Triumphant (CUT), an eclectic religious sect that has its international headquarters on a sprawling ranch north of Yellowstone. CUT followers annually gather near the park on a parcel of land they call the "Heart of the Inner Retreat." Church officials threatened to sue the National Park Service if the fire swept through their sacred religious grounds.

Above: Crews walk between hot spots along the fire line. Breathing the dense smoke is the equivalent of smoking four packs of cigarettes a day. JAMES WOODCOCK

Right: Fanned by high winds, fire sweeps up the edge of Grant Village in late July. The development was saved when firefighters used hoses to knock the flames out of the trees. LARRY MAYER

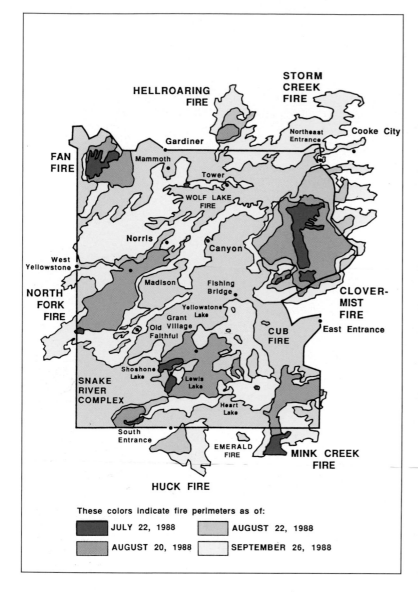

**STORM
CREEK
FIRE**

**HELLROARING
FIRE**

Cooke City

Gardiner
Northeast
Entrance

**FAN
FIRE**
Mammoth

Tower

WOLF LAKE
FIRE

Norris

Canyon

West
Yellowstone

Madison
Fishing
Bridge

Yellowstone
Lake

**CLOVER-
MIST
FIRE**

**NORTH
FORK
FIRE**

Grant
Village
Old
Faithful

East Entrance

**CUB
FIRE**

Shoshone
Lake

Lewis
Lake

**SNAKE
RIVER
COMPLEX**

Heart
Lake

South
Entrance

EMERALD
FIRE

**MINK CREEK
FIRE**

HUCK FIRE

These colors indicate fire perimeters as of:

■	JULY 22, 1988	▨	AUGUST 22, 1988
▨	AUGUST 20, 1988	□	SEPTEMBER 26, 1988

*This map shows the fires' progress throughout the summer in four
stages. The first stage shows the scope of the fires on July 22, when
firefighting efforts began on all fires. Aug. 20 was Black Saturday
when high winds fanned fires to new dimensions. The outside outline
shows the final fire perimeters.* MAP BY JOHN POTTER

Employees of TW Services, the park's major concessionaire, wait to be evacuated from Grant Village. Throughout the summer, employees were shuttled to different jobs in the park as fire closed facilities.
JAMES WOODCOCK

Firefighters rest after
spending hours building
fire lines, the grueling
job of clearing trails
through the forest in an
effort to stop the fire.
LARRY MAYER

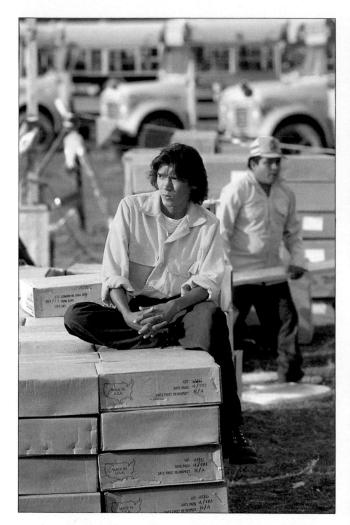

Meanwhile, sect leader Elizabeth Clare Prophet, whom followers call "Guru Ma," led 250 church members to a meadow near the encroaching fire, where they shouted high-speed chants to try to reverse the fire's spread. In a rapid-fire monotone unintelligible to an unpracticed ear, the members chanted, "Reverse the tide. Roll them back. Set all free." Firefighters already had stepped up their efforts along the park boundary near the CUT ranch, attacking the fire with additional crews and aircraft. Keeping fire off private property was a high priority.

The night after the CUT members chanted, the fire activity subsided and firefighters were able to hold the containment line along the boundary. Both the firefighters and the CUT members claimed credit for one of man's few successes against Yellowstone's 1988 fires.

CUT officials joined other residents of the region in assailing the National Park Service for initially allowing the fires to burn. Although the Park Service had said it was trying to put all the fires out as of July 22, many in the region continued to complain about the policy.

The fires were beginning to affect the tourism trade. Residents of smoke-choked gateway communities

Left: A mountain of provisions surrounds a firefighter at the supply camp at West Yellowstone. Supplying food and equipment to the thousands of firefighters in the field was a logistical challenge.
JAMES WOODCOCK

Above: Scott Park of Libby uses his pulaski to put out a spot fire near Grant Village. Pulaskis, hand tools which are a combination hoe and axe, are the firefighters' primary tool.
LARRY MAYER

were upset that a tourist season that had shown prom-ise was dwindling. Road closures created an obstacle course for tourist traffic.

Other tourists were fascinated by the fires. They lis-tened to Park Service naturalists talk about the role fire plays in the ecology of high-country forests. They snapped pictures and watched firefighting activity as if it were a regular attraction.

Firefighters, meanwhile, reported horror stories from the fire lines on just how tinder-dry the forests were

becoming. In one case, a downed log in the southern portion of the park was lit with a single match as part of a backburn. One firefighter said he watched as fire crept along the ground until it came to a standing lodge-pole. Within 30 seconds, the entire tree was engulfed in flames.

Dave Poncin, who was incident commander when the Red-Shoshone Fire invaded Grant Village, was called back to oversee the North Fork Fire in mid-August. He reported that, in the three weeks since he

was first called to Yellowstone, fire conditions had grown much more extreme. Meadows that once acted as barriers to fires had turned from green to brown and were now carrying flames.

During mid-August, the North Fork Fire swept around Madison Junction and jumped the Firehole, Gibbon and Madison rivers in one day, closing roads in the area. The fire prediction team had said the fire would not reach Madison Junction by the end of the month.

One member of the fire prediction team said later that the projections underestimated the fire's spread for several reasons. Fires were burning through all kinds of vegetation, including younger lodgepole stands that were not expected to carry the fires. The team also had not anticipated the unseasonable, unrelenting, high winds that fanned the fires. Later, other fire-behavior specialists working the fires doubled and quadrupled their projections to take into account the extremely dry conditions.

Extreme fire behavior was not limited to the park. On Aug. 16, Yellowstone's Assistant Superintendent Ben Clary and Chief Ranger Dan Sholly were on a helicopter reconnaissance flight near the north end of the park when they spotted a new fire burning in the Absaroka-Beartooth Wilderness of the Gallatin National Forest. The helicopter landed and Clary and Sholly worked to save an outfitter's camp next to where the fire was burning. They radioed for help and smokejumpers were flown to the scene, but could not parachute to the ground because of high winds.

Previous page: The Clover-Mist Fire casts an eerie glow by moonlight with Pilot Peak in the background.
BOB ZELLAR

Left: A B-26 bomber begins a retardant-dropping run on the North Fork Fire.
LARRY MAYER

*Manning a shovel, a
firefighter runs through
a meadow to extinguish
a spot fire.* BOB ZELLAR

Sholly and Clary manned shovels, but the fire grew too quickly. Within a day it covered 250 acres and, before the end of a week, had grown to more than 2,000 acres. The Hellroaring Fire was born.

Meanwhile the Clover-Mist Fire in the northeast corner of the park was pressing its way toward the Montana communities of Cooke City and Silver Gate. Residents accused the Park Service of taking inadequate action to stop the fire, then about 10 miles away. "Nobody likes to play with fire," one resident said.

As the fire activity grew, the face of Yellowstone changed. Campgrounds once occupied by recreational vehicles and tourists' tents became fire camps where firefighters slept and fire bosses planned and coordinated strategy. Caterers served thousands of meals to famished firefighters. Showers and portable telephones were brought to these impromptu cities. Computers in the back of cargo vans tracked the logistics of caring for fire crews.

The air over Yellowstone suddenly was full of helicopters and airplanes—a mainstay in forest firefighting efforts since the end of World War II. Heliports to service the dozens of helicopters popped up in open meadows where elk and bison usually graze.

The plethora of aircraft caused safety problems. Fire bosses threatened to shut down all air traffic in August after two incidents in which pilots had to take evasive action to miss other aircraft. They blamed the problems on pilots using different radio frequencies.

Fire bosses also preached safety to the firefighters on the ground, who had to take special precaution because of Yellowstone's special circumstances. Crews working in the park's back country had to keep an eye out for grizzly bears. They stored their garbage in bear-proof traps and flew it out of the area daily. A half-dozen firefighters were treated at a Yellowstone clinic after they inhaled sulfur gas while working around a hot spring. Other crews walked cautiously around thermal areas to keep from breaking through the thin crust next to hot pools.

By Aug. 19, the fires perimeters had spread over 282,000 acres. The ranks of firefighters had grown to more than 2,000. Firefighters were meeting with little success and said their only hope for gaining was rain, which hadn't fallen in a month, or a break in the wind. But relief did not arrive. In fact, the worst was yet to come.

Skies hazy with smoke
created spectacular
sunsets, such as this
one near Grant Village.
JAMES WOODCOCK

BLACK SATURDAY

Midnight approached on Aug. 19 while photographer Larry Mayer and reporter Robert Ekey stood near Beryl Hot Springs in Gibbon Canyon between Madison Junction and Norris. The spring belched a sulfur-laden mist into air already heavy with wood smoke from hundreds of small fires that dotted the canyon walls.

An arm of the North Fork Fire had swept through the area earlier in the day as it headed north toward Norris. After the winds died down and the temperature dropped, the fire was reduced to the spots glowing around the two journalists. Many were the size of campfires, some still as big as 20 feet in diameter. Occasionally flames flared through a patch of small trees, only to lie back down again, as if rousing in their sleep.

The fires sleeping on that Friday night awakened on Saturday morning to a high wind that quickly slapped them into action. By noon, the small, seemingly harmless campfires joined and grew into a monster with flames 200 feet tall, sweeping toward Norris in an angry firestorm hungry for more fuel to maintain its fierce existence.

Mother Nature flexed her muscle that morning. Winds sustained themselves at 30 to 40 miles per hour and gusted to 70 miles per hour. Trees blew down and fires grew so fierce that they created their own wind. Mammoth flames reached far above the treetops and arched with the wind, like a giant wave ready to crash down on the forest below.

By midmorning, the strong winds grounded helicopters and airplanes. The fires grew so intense that all attempts to slow them were futile. Firefighters could work only in a

A backfire lit by fire crews consumes pines near Silver Gate. This strategy failed to stop the advance of the main fire, and the backfire itself eventually burned out of control. BOB ZELLAR

few isolated areas to protect buildings—and helplessly watch the roaring fires.

Weather forecasters had predicted a "red-flag day" that Saturday with winds faster than 20 miles per hour, hot temperatures and low humidity. But the weather and its results surprised even the most experienced firefighters. They never had seen so much sustained wind in a wildfire.

By midnight of Aug. 20—dubbed "Black Saturday"—fires throughout the Yellowstone region had consumed an additional 165,000 acres of forest land, growing by more than 50 percent in a single day. Every fire in the area made major runs. Fires that had been smoldering sprang to life and new starts quickly became major fires. Black Saturday forever changed firefighters' perceptions of fire activity in the Yellowstone region. They realized the futility of trying to stop fires at their fronts and just how explosive fire conditions were.

The intense fire caused chaos in Yellowstone. Roads closed, stranding tourists. Dozens of firefighters had to flee the flames.

Yellowstone Superintendent Robert Barbee attended a meeting at West Yellowstone that morning and later found the direct route back to park headquarters in Mammoth closed by fire. He took the roundabout route and ran into more fire. In midafternoon Barbee found himself at West Thumb in south-central Yellowstone, helping rangers hastily evacuate tourists as the Red-Shoshone Fire made a run at the development.

Similar scenes were played out throughout the greater Yellowstone region that day. Fires crossed roads, separating tourists from their hotel rooms. Travelers dashed along roads past uncontrolled wildfire to escape from the park's flaming interior.

The fires would have other hot days, but none that saw fires grow as quickly as on Black Saturday. "On Saturday, we could have had the entire United States Army in here and it wouldn't have made any difference," Barbee said.

Above: Frustrated fire bosses huddle to discuss strategy as fires continue to sweep across fire lines and ignore man's attempts to slow them.
JAMES WOODCOCK

Right: Firefighters hose down the roof of the Norris Museum. They feared the fires would shower embers on the shake roof.
LARRY MAYER

Mayer, *The Billings Gazette*'s chief photographer, and Ekey, *The Gazette*'s Bozeman reporter, spent the day with firefighters watching the North Fork Fire. Fire officials had anticipated an active day, but were caught by surprise when the winds kicked up well before noon. A planned 1 p.m. closure of the highway inside the western edge of the park that links Norris and Madison Junction was quickly moved up and rangers in patrol cars used loudspeakers to hustle tourists out of the area.

Near Elk Flats, fire swept through treetops and threatened to cross the highway. The *Gazette* journalists moved north of the fire, toward Norris, and stood with fire officials watching the inferno, vehicles idling in the roadway. Wind gusts to 60 miles per hour snapped trees in the forest around them. Thick, gray smoke was pouring over their heads as they watched and waited.

As it nears, a wildfire creates much the same sensation as an approaching train. First you hear—almost feel—a distant rumble. Puffs of black smoke appear in the columns of gray—a sign of greater burning intensity—and the sound of the fire increases. Then whiffs of air hit the back of your neck as you face the fire, evidence that the fire is creating its own wind, sucking oxygen from along the ground to sustain itself, then blowing it thousands of feet into the air in a boiling column of smoke.

As the inferno nears, it roars like a jet engine as the blaze sucks more and more air. You can feel the heat and see the flames half a mile away. Thick smoke occasionally obscures the blaze and the noise dissipates for a moment as the flames gasp momentarily for air before making their next leap.

Man always has regarded fire, in its undisciplined form, as evil and destructive. But the unbridled fury of wildfire raging through a forest also creates a sense of awe and a fascination for nature at work.

As the two journalists stood with a dozen fire officials on Black Saturday, southwesterly winds pushed the roaring blaze along the roadway past them. A quick shift in the wind direction suddenly brought the flames directly toward the group and sent people scrambling for their vehicles. Even inside the vehicles, the heat was as intense as if someone had left the car heater on in the middle of summer.

Through thick smoke that cut visibility to 25 yards, the group eased northward toward Norris, listening for the telltale roar, feeling for the heat and peering into the grayness for the dark-orange glow that would tell that the fire was near.

At Norris, a dozen firefighters and rangers gathered to try to protect the historic log museum that overlooks the geyser basins there. The steaming, barren geyser basins stood as a substantial barrier between the museum and the raging fire, but firefighters worried that a thin band of trees could carry the fire close enough to drop embers on the museum's shake roof. A pair of firefighters hosed down the roof of the small museum building while the others took up positions

near the forest and prepared to knock the approaching flames out of the treetops.

As the inevitable inferno approached, flames 200 feet tall burned to within 150 yards of the museum. The heat, even through the dense smoke and steam from geysers, was searing. Above the approaching roar came what sounded like rifle shots as trees exploded in the intense heat. Rangers took bearings on barren "safe spots" in the geyser basin in case they needed to flee from the fire.

Firefighters are trained to keep a safe spot in mind at all times and go there if a fire overtakes them. In addition, they wear flame-retardant clothing and carry fire shelters—thick, foil, one-person tents they can crawl into to escape a fire. Firefighters learn to lie on barren ground and pull the shelter over themselves. People who have used fire shelters say they can get hot enough to burn flesh, so firefighters wear gloves to protect their hands as they pull the tents over their heads.

Though firefighters call the shelters "brown-and-serve bags," they are credited with saving dozens of lives. During the 1988 Yellowstone fires, more than four dozen people deployed fire shelters.

Left: Flames shoot hundreds of feet above the trees as a firestorm sweeps forward, generating its own wind and weather. BOB ZELLAR

Above: A firefighter douses a spot fire caused when high winds carried burning embers miles ahead of a firestorm approaching the Norris Museum. LARRY MAYER

Previous page: Hundreds of small fires smolder along the Gibbon River on the eve of Black Saturday. The next day, wind whipped the fires into a firestorm. LARRY MAYER

Above: Fire bosses monitor the North Fork Fire as it rages along the highway south of Norris on Black Saturday. Thousands of acres went up in smoke that day. LARRY MAYER

There was no need to use the fire shelters at Norris on Black Saturday. The fire stopped at the edge of the geyser basin. Another finger of flames later ran past Norris and burned toward other developments.

The gale-force winds of Black Saturday pushed glowing embers forward. Spotting, like all other fire activity, was at its worst. On Black Saturday, airborne embers landed as far as a mile and a half ahead of the fires. The embers started fires with incredible frequency—in some instances every time one landed. With fuel moisture levels and humidity at record lows and temperatures in the 80s, the spots smoldered only minutes before bursting into flames.

The spot fires grew in size as they were pulled toward the main fire by fire-induced drafts. Continuing to grow in size and intensity, they drew the main fire toward themselves, creating a pulsating action between the two fires, causing both to intensify. When the fires eventually joined, they released even more energy. The proliferation of spot fires created dangerous situations for firefighters who had to be cautious not to get trapped between two fires.

Until Aug. 20, 1988, fire officials generally could count on fires burning most actively in the late afternoon, after the sun warmed the air and relative humidity dropped. As evening approached and temperatures fell, the fires would lie down for the night.

On the evening of Black Saturday it was obvious that the fires were not about to lie down. Mayer and Ekey decided to leave Norris before the fast-moving fires cut off the only remaining escape route to Mammoth. Already, the fires had closed two roads behind them. The journalists also knew that the spectacular fire activity they witnessed that afternoon was not limited just to the Norris area.

As Mayer and Ekey drove north toward Mammoth, the smoke cleared, revealing huge cumulus clouds perched atop towering smoke columns to the east and northeast, signs that the Hellroaring, Storm Creek and Clover-Mist fires also had exploded that day. To the south, above Norris, the smoke from which the journalists emerged pushed up to 30,000 feet, obliterating from view other smoke columns where new fires had started south of Yellowstone.

Just south of the Yellowstone boundary, wind had pushed a tree across a power line, sparking fire in a thick lodgepole pine stand littered with downed timber. The fire grew 4,000 acres in just two hours—tes-

*Yellowstone Park officials
discuss the intense fire
activity of Black Saturday as
they stand silhouetted against
the flame-colored sky.*
LARRY MAYER

timony to the extreme burning conditions that day. Called the Huck Fire, it expanded so rapidly that rangers had to move quickly to evacuate the Flagg Ranch and clear the J.D. Rockefeller Parkway, linking Yellowstone to Grand Teton National Park to the south. The fire roared toward Yellowstone National Park.

At 2 p.m. an aspen tree blew over a power line starting the Hunter Fire in Grand Teton National Park. By 8:30 that night the fire had charred 2,000 acres.

The Clover-Mist Fire, in the wilderness along Yellowstone's eastern boundary, burned an additional 55,000 acres on Black Saturday as it raced toward Cooke City. Its huge column of smoke spooked residents of the picturesque tourist town, many of whom made plans to evacuate.

The Hellroaring Fire, which had started several days before north of Yellowstone in the Absaroka-Beartooth

Wilderness area, lived up to its name that day, running an average of one mile per hour for eight hours.

Northeast of Yellowstone, the Storm Creek Fire, also in the Absaroka-Beartooth Wilderness, had been smoldering for weeks. On Black Saturday it made an astonishing 10-mile run—astonishing because of its size

---

Above: Firefighters built more than 850 miles of fire lines in the greater Yellowstone area during the summer of 1988. Only a few miles successfully held back the flames.
LARRY MAYER

Right: Black Saturday's fire activity filled the sky with huge smoke columns often capped with thunderheads. The smoke spread across the region, dropping ash on communities up to 100 miles away.
LARRY MAYER

*Tourists race to beat the
fire that was threatening
to jump the road south
of Norris. Roads closed
by fire often disrupted
tourist traffic.*
LARRY MAYER

and because it ran south, against the prevailing winds and in the opposite direction of all the other fires.

The Storm Creek Fire, which had burned only 5,500 acres since it started in mid-June, ballooned to 23,680 acres. Fire behavior specialists were puzzled that the Storm Creek Fire moved against the prevailing winds. One expert speculated that the fire was drawn south by winds generated by the huge Clover-Mist Fire, 10 miles away. Other specialists contended that the prevailing wind reversed itself after crossing a high ridge, creating an eddy of air that swept the fire south.

The Storm Creek fire's advance toward Cooke City narrowed the isthmus of unburned timber surround-

ing the tiny Montana town at Yellowstone's northeast gate. But, residents did not realize the Storm Creek Fire had charged toward them from the north. They were preoccupied with the thundering tower of smoke that spread over their mountain community from the Clover-Mist fire to the southwest.

For days, residents of Cooke City and nearby Silver Gate had complained that the Clover-Mist Fire threatened them. But Yellowstone officials continued to assure them that the blaze would be contained. On Black Saturday, the Clover-Mist Fire ran to within four miles of the communities, held back only by a high ridge.

Charred embers from the Clover-Mist Fire dropped

into Cooke City as residents wondered whether the fire would stop at the ridge or run into their tourist town, which is laden with old log buildings.

Smoke exhaled by the Yellowstone fires on Black Saturday sent giant plumes across northern Wyoming, southern Montana and into the Midwest. Ash fell on Billings, 60 miles northeast of the fires. It took little skill to interpret the smoke signals: The Yellowstone fires had entered a new dimension.

More than any other day in the summer of 1988, Black Saturday forced firefighters to change the way they looked at fire. Traditional strategies and tactics were obsolete this year. Nature was at work and was prevailing.

Frames of reference changed. In one day, nearly five times as much acreage burned in Yellowstone as in the previous 16 years combined.

Startled by the day's events, park officials and fire bosses put out a call for help. Additional top-level fire-management teams were summoned to oversee efforts at the Clover-Mist, Hunter, Storm Creek and Hellroaring fires.

Dozens of additional 20-person crews were called in. More helicopters and air tankers were requested. Fire managers met until after midnight to assess the day's events and map new strategy. Those who slept at all arose before dawn to brief fire crews.

Yellowstone's top officials met until nearly midnight on Black Saturday debating whether to close the park. Tourists had been exposed to wildfire or stranded when fire closed roads between them and their hotel reservations. The officials decided to close the interior of the park until fires subsided. Tourists could see Old Faithful if they entered from West Yellowstone, but travel elsewhere in the park was limited.

Before Black Saturday, park employees already had put in a month of long hours trying to safely mix tourism and the firefighting effort. Frayed nerves and fatigue already were beginning to show.

Late that night, there was a sense of realization among everyone in Yellowstone that the fire season was far from over. In fact, it had just begun on a far grander scale than anyone had ever fathomed.

There would be more red-flag days, more wind and many more acres burned. A quarter-million acres would burn in three days. Fire officials would be forced to direct their limited resources at protecting buildings, leaving other wildfires to burn.

The nightmare, it seemed, had only begun.

Above: Nature's awesome, unbridled fury humbled firefighters for more than three months. BOB ZELLAR

Next page: On some days, smoke was so dense at the West Yellowstone Airport that aircraft were grounded, hampering firefighting activities.

LARRY MAYER

A NIGHTMARE THAT WOULDN'T END

In the wake of Black Saturday, forest fires swept unchecked across the Yellowstone area as firefighters mounted a massive effort. Firefighters from as far away as Hawaii and Florida were called to the Yellowstone high country. The military was called in to supplement civilian crews and the first Army infantry troops arrived on Aug. 22.

Weather was the firefighters' nemesis, as constant winds sent wildfires sprinting across the parched landscape. Forest Service rangers manned helicopters and rode horses into the back country to evacuate people from the path of approaching fire.

Inversions became a daily occurrence, shrouding the park and gateway communities in a blanket of acrid smoke each morning. Adding to the atmosphere of gloom, convoys of civilian and Army firefighters shuttled across the park. With the troops moving to the battle lines and constant helicopter and airplane traffic, Yellowstone more closely resembled a war zone than the nation's premier national park.

As tourism dwindled, the park's concessionaire closed the Lake Hotel. Fire did not threaten the Lake development yet, but thick smoke blocked the view across the lake. Tourists went to bed breathing the smoke and awoke each morning breathing an even stronger stench. Park officials warned tourists with respiratory problems to reconsider their vacation plans.

Like the pall of smoke that covered the park, a sense of frustration and fatalism hung in the air. The massive firefighting effort seemed futile in the face of nature's rage. "It's a nightmare that won't end," one Park Service employee said.

A fireball explodes skyward after a dry hillside erupts in flames east of Cooke City.
JAMES WOODCOCK

Fires spread despite natural barriers or sparse fuels. Daily fire advances were measured in miles and thousands of acres. The North Fork Fire had swept past Norris and its 200-foot-tall flames lapped at the edge of Canyon Village, forcing the evacuation of tourists. Cooke City and Silver Gate, at the park's northeastern corner, were spared by the Clover-Mist Fire, but the Storm Creek Fire to the north loomed over the tiny mountain communities.

Fire officials compared the fires to the "Big Blow-up" of 1910, when a giant wildfire burned 3 million acres of Idaho and Montana forests in 48 hours.

No significant rain had fallen on the Yellowstone area since early July, and the fire conditions worsened. Throughout the northern Rocky Mountains and the

Pacific Northwest, major fires burned. In Yellowstone, the number of firefighters approached 9,000, but the Interagency Fire Center in Boise, Idaho, wanted as many as 1,000 of them and some aircraft to fight other fires. At an Aug. 26 meeting of fire bosses for the 11 major fires burning in the Yellowstone area, forest supervisors and park officials argued that they could not spare crews.

Ultimately, more military, supervised by experienced firefighters, were assigned to relieve civilian crews in Yellowstone.

The extreme burning conditions prompted a significant shift in strategy. Firefighters' priorities shifted to containing three small fires that already were under control. New fires were aggressively attacked. Efforts to stop the larger fires head-on became secondary to protecting communities. Back-country fires that did not threaten buildings were allowed to run their courses.

The changes in strategy marked a change in outlook. Fire bosses no longer were optimistic that they could contain the blazes. Fire-behavior specialists offered worst-case scenarios and the first projections that the fires could spread to more than 1 million acres—half of Yellowstone National Park.

The moisture level of some logs fell to 7 percent—nearly half that of kiln-dried lumber. Brush, grasses and twigs were measured at 3 percent and 5 percent moisture. At between 8 percent and 12 percent moisture, fires burn freely. Young vegetation burned with ease, something never before witnessed in the region.

Fire officials were disturbed that fuel moisture levels did not rise at night. Normally, as temperature drops the relative humidity rises and the forest absorbs moisture from the air. Fires usually burn most intensely during the late afternoon, when fuel is dried by the sun. They normally subside at night when the moisture levels rise. During Yellowstone's summer of fire, the fuel moisture levels remained low around the clock. Crown fires at midnight left an ominous orange glow in the sky. Firefighting was suspended at night, however, because of the danger.

Dry cold fronts periodically passed through the area, preceded by two days of high winds. Radical fire behavior became a daily occurrence.

Areas within Yellowstone created their own microclimates. Winds blowing southward, up the Grand Canyon of the Yellowstone and against the prevailing

U.S. Army infantry troops await transportation to Yellowstone Park after arriving in Bozeman. They were the first of 4,400 soldiers and Marines flown in to fight the fires. LARRY MAYER

wind direction, frustrated firefighters trying to protect Canyon Village.

Nighttime downslope winds pushed the North Fork Fire closer to West Yellowstone, against the daytime prevailing winds. The downslope winds, caused by the air cooling at higher elevations in the heart of Yellowstone and drifting down from the high plateau, also brought smoke that hung in the air until midday.

Smoke plumes drifting from fires on the western side of Yellowstone shaded the eastern half of the park, dropping temperatures and substantially reducing fire activity there.

On the rare still days, the fires created their own wind and expanded in all directions, sometimes breaking through fire lines that had held for weeks.

In late August, the southern flank of the North Fork Fire broke over a containment line that had held for a

month, and renewed its threat to Old Faithful. Although it still was eight miles away from the world-famous geyser basin, winds pushed the fire through dense forests of lodgepole pines killed by mountain bark pine beetles. Dave Poncin, incident commander of the North Fork Fire, called the fire's renewed vigor "humbling"—something he hadn't seen before. By then, however, fire bosses were growing accustomed to expecting the unusual.

Fire behavior was so unprecedented that firefighting guidelines were rewritten. Firefighters' perceptions of forest fires changed as well. One 15,000-acre blowup across fire lines on the North Fork Fire was called a "slopover." Flanks and rears of fires became fire fronts. Five- and 10-mile advances of fires in one day were predicted and expected. Fires easily jumped the gaping Grand Canyon of the Yellowstone and the barren Old Faithful geyser basin.

As the end of August approached, fire bosses had to lobby the command center at West Yellowstone for more resources. Commanders had to fight to keep other fires in the nation from siphoning off their men and equipment.

William Penn Mott, director of the National Park Service, toured Yellowstone and said he was surprised by the extent of the fires. They had burned 660,000 acres in the Yellowstone area, with about two-thirds of that in the national park. Fire commanders told Mott

Left: Two firefighters prepare to spray the roof of the historic Old Faithful Inn as fire threatens the area. Nearly 700 guests in the inn were told to leave earlier that day.
JUDY TELL

Above: A Yellowstone employee helps confused tourists route their trip through the park when the fires forced the closure of many developments and roads. LARRY MAYER

*TW Services employee
Sue Harn shields her
face from flying ash and
embers as the firestorm
hits the Old Faithful
complex.* JUDY TELL

that another dry cold front would move across the area soon, sparking more wind and more extreme fire activity.

The next day high winds sent fires across containment lines again and the perimeters of fires grew to surround 20 percent of the park. The North Fork Fire became so large that the commanders divided supervision of efforts against it into two camps. The northeastern half of the fire was renamed the Wolf Lake Fire.

Burning south of Canyon and near Hayden Valley, in the center of Yellowstone National Park, the Wolf Lake Fire jumped the Yellowstone River and began burning toward the Clover-Mist Fire, which had roared

across the park's eastern boundary and into the Shoshone National Forest, forcing evacuation of two ranches along the Clarks Fork River.

As September approached, firefighters battled a new enemy—fatigue. Some crews were on the fire lines for weeks with little relief. Fire bosses constantly preached safety as their crews faced danger daily. Snags—burned trees still standing—could fall quietly with no warning. Chain saws and even sharp hand tools posed dangers to the weary crews. At the end of August, however, no serious injuries had been reported from the firefighting effort, despite the large build-up of forces. But there were hundreds of minor injuries and smoke-related illnesses. Breathing the smoke on the front lines was like smoking four packs of cigarettes a day.

For the crews, the day's assignment often included hours of scraping the earth bare near the fires with pulaskis—firefighting tools that are half hoe and half axe. Looking much like a hiking trail, these fire lines are designed to stop a ground fire. They were ineffective in Yellowstone, however, as the fire swept through the treetops or spotted over the lines. At one point, 400 miles of fire line were in place. When the winds came up, only 20 miles held.

The lack of success frustrated firefighters and their

Left: A helicopter drops water on fires sweeping toward Silver Gate. Helicopters dropped 10 million gallons of water on the 13 major fires in Yellowstone.
JAMES WOODCOCK

Above: Fireman Dan Bell of Victor, Mont , hoses down a Cooke City cafe as part of an all-out effort to save the town.
JAMES WOODCOCK

*A satellite image shows a smoke plume drifting across
northern Wyoming, southern Montana, Nebraska, North and
South Dakota (states outlined in black). The photo was
taken on Sept. 7, a day when high winds fanned fires
throughout the park.* COURTESY USGS EROS DATA CENTER

*Above: Park employees
huddle near the Old
Faithful geyser, seeking
refuge from the firestorm
sweeping down on the
park's most popular tourist
attraction.* JUDY TELL

bosses. Poncin, the commander for the North Fork Fire, had spent five weeks directing firefighters in Yellowstone. The North Fork Fire grew despite his best efforts. "You don't like to walk away from a fire with the smoke column as large as when you arrived," he said.

Residents of the region also were weary of the fire and constant smoke. Despite the massive firefighting effort, they maintained the perception that the park's "let-it-burn" policy still was in effect. Only a half-hearted effort was being made to extinguish the blazes, they thought.

Angry residents directed their frustration directly at Yellowstone Superintendent Robert Barbee. He had held controversial posts in the Park Service before, but this was the first time he had been subjected to such personal attack, including one West

Yellowstone motel marquee that said, "Welcome to the Barbee-que." Some of the attacks came from people who operate tourism businesses and who wondered whether tourism ever would recover. Others reacted emotionally to fire running rampant through the magnificent landscape that held some personal attachment.

To quell the sharp criticism, top regional directors of the National Park Service and U.S. Forest Service conducted a press conference over Labor Day weekend to explain the extreme fire conditions and the efforts to stop the fires. They also carried another message—another dry cold front was forecast. That would mean that another quarter million acres could burn in Yellowstone in the next three days. Their predictions soon became reality.

The fire season climaxed during the first 10 days of September. Rampant flames swept across the landscape, so wide and full that avoiding towns and buildings seemed impossible. Flames swept up to, around or over nearly every development inside Yellowstone and threatened communities just outside its boundaries.

The Clover-Mist Fire, 25 miles wide and 30 miles long, swept down drainages toward cabins and ranches tucked into the forest in the Crandall Creek and

Sunlight Basin areas east of the park. Downslope winds blew the North Fork Fire two miles toward West Yellowstone on the night of Sept. 1, throwing an eerie orange glow in the sky above the town. Residents filled their cars with gasoline, loaded valuables and prepared to flee. The fire stopped a mile and a quarter from town.

Fire crews manning engines, many from volunteer fire departments throughout Montana and Wyoming, were assigned to protect towns and buildings from the onslaught.

On Sept. 1, a firefighter described the Storm Creek Fire northeast of Yellowstone as "burning like a freight train at 9 p.m.," as it chugged toward Cooke City and Silver Gate. Two days later, the fire roared through the historic Silvertip Ranch, an exclusive, private guest ranch along Yellowstone's northern boundary. Three dozen firefighters deployed fire shelters as the blaze swept past them. Remarkably, there were no injuries and no buildings burned.

In the path of the Storm Creek Fire, Cooke City and Silver Gate residents were evacuated. Bulldozers gashed a huge fire line through the forest near Yel-

lowstone's northeast entrance in an effort to stop the blaze.

Fire bosses decided to defend the towns by waiting for favorable winds, then lighting a backfire. They calculated that a backfire would burn toward the Storm Creek Fire and scorch an area that would starve the advancing inferno. Without the backburn, they feared that the Storm Creek Fire could roar through the communities.

The backfire was lit and watched for two days. Then the wind shifted and an ember from the backfire crossed the bulldozed fire line. The wind whipped the small spot fire into a wall of flame that swept toward

*Above: Denny Bungarz,
fire boss of the North
Fork Fire, conducts a
tour of the park for
Interior Secretary
Donald Hodel and
Wyoming Governor Mike
Sullivan.* LARRY MAYER

Silver Gate. The fire later moved north of Silver Gate and Cooke City, spreading east toward Cooke Pass and destroying several homes and cabins. Ironically, the Storm Creek Fire never burned into the backfire.

On Sept. 6, the perimeters of the Yellowstone area fires exceeded 1 million acres and they still raged out of control. "Mother Nature is making the decisions here," one spokeswoman said.

Gary Cargill, the U.S. Forest Service's Rocky Mountain regional forester, applauded the efforts of firefighters, despite the disappointments. "They are crack firefighters who are not used to getting whipped day after day."

The firefighting effort had swollen to 9,500 people and 117 aircraft, including the Army's huge Chinook helicopters. Eleven of the nation's most experienced fire-management teams supervised the 13 named fires in the Yellowstone area. Fire danger grew so extreme in Montana that the governor banned all outdoor recreation. Smoke continued to pour out of the park, exceeding healthy levels in many gateway communities.

Meanwhile, the threat to Old Faithful loomed again. Fire that had slopped over a month-old containment line on the southern tip of the North Fork Fire had marched seven miles and was within a mile of Old Faithful on the night of Sept. 6. Park officials decided to evacuate the 700 guests at the historic Old Faithful Inn the next morning. Bellhops knocked on doors and asked guests to leave in an orderly evacuation.

The fire burned closer throughout the morning and early afternoon, separated from the historic geyser basin and 400-building town by only a low ridge. A huge smoke column billowed over the development as a steady stream of air tankers dropped retardant on the leading edge of the fire and helicopters dipped

Right: Tourists study a road map after being forced to evacuate the Old Faithful Inn. The historic inn was not damaged by fire.
BOB ZELLAR

Next page: Flames consume one of the 16 buildings destroyed when the North Fork Fire overran the Old Faithful complex. Most of the buildings were small cabins. ROBERT EKEY

water buckets from a sewage treatment lagoon that had been filled with fresh water.

In midafternoon, winds picked up and the fire crested the ridge a quarter of a mile from Old Faithful. Heat radiated to the parking lot. Tourists and concessionaire employees still in the area, some approaching hysteria, were shepherded from the area by a park ranger in a patrol car.

Suddenly the wind shifted and strengthened and the fierce firestorm swept down onto Old Faithful in a matter of minutes. Firefighters assigned to protect government housing on the edge of the village had to retreat hastily from the flames. Wind blew thick, brown smoke into the village and sent glowing embers the size of golf balls skidding across the pavement.

Firestorms have rolling action, burning so intensely that the heat alone can set a building on fire. At Old

Faithful, as the fire rolled in, flying embers landed on building roofs. Sixteen small cabins and a storage shed burned as firefighters dashed around the development trying to put out small fires. A deluge system was activated on the Old Faithful Inn, wetting the roof and saving the historic log hotel. Denny Bungarz, the North Fork Fire boss who often offered an optimistic outlook, got a fire shelter out of the trunk of his car during the height of the firestorm.

An ember, which apparently had flown over the village and geyser basin, landed on a hillside half a mile from the nearest fire and ignited the forest. Within a minute, it swept 100 yards through the timber.

Ken Dittmer, commander for all of the fires in the Yellowstone area, said later that a wind shift of 2 or 3 degrees to the south could have meant disaster for the entire village, including the inn. "No amount of engines or water would have made any difference. We were right on the ragged edge," he said.

Bungarz said that Old Faithful no longer was threatened by the North Fork Fire—it already had

Left: A seemingly endless stream of firefighters marches to the front lines of the Clover-Mist Fire. Thousands of firefighters battled the 387,000-acre fire.
BOB ZELLAR

Above: A U.S. Marine from Camp Pendleton, Calif., surveys the fire scene near Mammoth. Toward the end of the Yellowstone firefighting effort, troops relieved civilian fire crews.
LARRY MAYER

Right: Cooke City residents gather to listen to Park Service reports about fires approaching their mountain community.
LARRY MAYER

burned around the area—but that the fire had thwarted all efforts to stop or slow it. "We threw everything at that fire from Day One," he said. "We tried everything we knew of or could think of,

Left: Despite widespread fire activity, many tourists carried on normal activities, including fishing in the Firehole River while fires burn on the opposite shore.
LARRY MAYER

Above: Fire on the hillside behind Cooke City threatened to engulf the gateway community.
JAMES WOODCOCK

and that fire kicked our ass from one end of the park to the other."

The same day saw intense fire activity in other areas. The Clover-Mist Fire burned 13 mobile homes and a store in the Crandall Creek area east of Yellowstone, where 50 homes had been evacuated. Four buildings were burned in Cooke Pass, victims of the backfire that raged out of control. The Wolf Lake Fire sent embers into Canyon Village and started a major run toward Mammoth and the park's headquarters. The threat to other towns had decreased as the fires swept around them. Protecting Mammoth, home to many park employees, became a priority.

As the fires raged, President Ronald Reagan dispatched cabinet officials to Yellowstone on a fact-

finding mission. Interior Secretary Donald Hodel, Agriculture Secretary Richard Lyng and Undersecretary of Defense William Taft arrived with the park and the region under siege by the massive fires. Five communities along the park boundaries were evacuated and fire still burned on the outskirts of nearly every development inside the park. The cabinet officers said they were shocked by the extent of the fires. The promised more help from the military and a review of the Park Service and Forest Service fire-management policy.

The firefighting effort was costing $3 million a day and already had totaled $89 million.

When the cabinet officials arrived on Sept. 11, there was another arrival—the first significant rain since July. The next morning, snow blanketed the park with a dusting in some areas and ankle-deep in others. Firefighters finally got the break they had hoped for all summer. For the next week, light precipitation fell on and off in the region, slowing the fires. U.S. Marines arrived to help with the effort. The end, it seemed, was near. But officials characterized the fires as sleep-

ing giants that could spring back to life if the rain stopped.

Democratic presidential candidate Michael Dukakis visited the park on Sept. 16, trying to capitalize on the national attention given to the fires. Hundreds of reporters now covered the fires, in turn attracting a procession of VIPs who took fire bosses away from the fire lines for briefings.

Fall was coming to the high country and, with it, moisture and cooler temperatures that slowed the fires. On Sept. 17, fire commanders cautiously said they had

---

Above: A volunteer fire department truck stands by to protect a building in Silver Gate as the Storm Creek Fire rages north of town.
JAMES WOODCOCK

Right: Old Faithful geyser erupts against a smoke cloud hours before a firestorm swept through the area.
BOB ZELLAR

turned the corner on the Yellowstone fires. For the first time in two months, talk turned to containing the blazes.

The firefighting effort tapered off quickly as crews, mostly military, worked to mop up hot spots. Of 5,500 firefighters in the region, 4,000 were Army infantry or Marines. Crews found themselves in the ironic

Above: Soldiers build a fire line near Old Faithful in one of many frustratingly futile attempts to stem the tide of fires. JUDY TELL

Right: Marines hike along the Gardner River after a day on the fire lines near Mammoth. LARRY MAYER

situation of fighting to keep warm in light snow and cold rain while fighting forest fires. The fires continued to burn on dry days, but daily advances were small.

Though safety continued to be a priority, the fires took their first life in September, killing a firefighter with a falling snag during mop-up operations. A second snag seriously injured another firefighter, and a pilot escaped injury when his helicopter landed upside down in a lake east of Yellowstone.

Firefighters worked into late October mopping up the fires, while other crews started rehabilitation of areas scarred by firefighting. Fire crews doused the last fires in late October, ending three months of battle.

The fires touched 793,880 acres—about 36 percent—of Yellowstone National Park, according to a detailed study of satellite images. About 1.4 million

*Above: Firefighters build
backfires near the park's
northeast entrance as
they try to burn up fuel
in the path of an
approaching blaze.*
BOB ZELLAR

*Right: Soldiers crowd
around a camp stove as
the first snow of the
year falls on the park.
The September snowfall
marked the beginning
of the end of the
historic fire season.*
LARRY MAYER

acres burned in the Yellowstone region. In about a third of the burned-over area, trees were untouched. Those areas would turn green in the spring.

In the Yellowstone area, the fires burned three houses, 13 mobile homes, 10 private cabins, two Forest Service cabins, a Park Service cabin and 18 cabins in Yellowstone that were leased or owned by the park's concessionaire.

During the $140 million effort, firefighters dug more than 850 miles of fire line by hand. Some 600 miles of that was around the North Fork Fire. Bulldozers scraped an additional 137 miles of fire lines, including 32 miles in Yellowstone. More than 1.4 million gallons of retardant were dropped from aerial tankers, and helicopters dropped an estimated 10 million gallons of water. More than 18,000 hours of aircraft time were logged over the park.

As the fall storms washed the skies clear of the dreary smoke that had hung over the region for most of the late summer, park vistas began to reappear and Yellowstone seemed a much different place. Fall colors mixed with the blackened forests in a vivid contrast. The pessimistic mood that had prevailed in the region turned to optimism.

From a tourist's point of view, most of the fire damage is in the back country, out of sight of roads. Driving through constant blackened forest is rare. The fires, instead, left a mosaic of black and green.

When the smoke was thick, it was difficult to assess the fire's damage. As the smoke cleared, people saw that it was not as bad as they feared.

Some businesses in gateway communities made up what they may had lost in tourist trade by catering to firefighters. They also saw the need to spread the word that Yellowstone was not devastated. There had been extensive burning, but the fires had not affected the geysers or wildlife, the major attractions in the park.

Yellowstone's landscape began to renew itself, and the healing process seemed to extend to the residents of the region as well.

Above: Snow covers a rural volunteer fireman and his convertible truck at Mammoth. The snow was a sign that soon he would be driving his truck home.

BOB ZELLAR

Next page: A military C-130 tanker drops a load of retardant on the North Fork Fire near West Yellowstone. A total of 1.4 million gallons of retardant were dropped on the Yellowstone fires.

LARRY MAYER

RENEWAL OF THE FOREST

Burned lodgepole pines still watch over Old Faithful geyser, although the nearest hill has more green forest than black. Ashes of September 1988 have been succeeded by seasons of scattered grasses and wildflowers.

Undisturbed by the fires, the famous geyser and the park's 10,000 other thermal features continue to churn, boil and explode on a landscape changed by fires and still changing because of them.

Nature covered Yellowstone's burned grasslands with greenery within a year, but in the forest land, some black lodgepole trunks will stand for decades. More timber land than meadow burned in 1988, and it will take half a century or more to regrow those forests.

Part of the burned national forest lands outside the park were logged, and parts—logged and unlogged—were replanted with tree seedlings.

Inside Yellowstone Park, nature alone has replanted forests burned in 1988. There was no reseeding or replanting park forests, said Yellowstone biologist Don Despain.

The National Park Service did relandscape in developed areas and it cut down some burned trees deemed to be safety hazards along roads, trails and picnic grounds. A contractor hauled them to a mill.

Lodgepole pine that burned so well in "dog-hair" thick stands in 1988, is growing back in even greater concentrations. Despain found lodgepole seedlings growing in densities of hundreds of thousands per acre in parts of the park. Even in spots that burned the hottest, researchers have counted at least one pine seedling per 12 square yards.

Lodgepole pines, sprouted from seeds released when the

A spectacular sunset over Yellowstone Park ends another hectic day for firefighters. BOB ZELLAR

fires' heat opened the serotinous cones, stand a few feet tall in some parts of the park. Elsewhere, the new trees are only several inches high. Soil type and available moisture make the difference.

The fires of 1988 burned with such intensity in some places that stands of relatively young—10 to 20 year old—trees were consumed, according to Despain.

The oldest trees that burned in 1988 were 512 years old, Despain said. All of the ancient pines forming the forest canopy—the high covering of interlocking branches that had shaded the forest floor—were hundreds of years old. That canopy may be restored 40 to 50 years after the fires. By then 30- to 40-foot trees may be tall enough for their branches to come together to close the forest canopy again.

The changing forest has drawn hundreds of scientists to Yellowstone since the fires. They have studied animals, forests and waterways, finding new and sometimes surprising interrelationships in the Yellowstone ecosystem.

"There had not been a fire of the magnitude and scope of the Yellowstone fires since there's been a science of ecology," said John Varley, chief of the park's resource center. "The last really big ones in the Rocky Mountains were in 1910 and that was before there was an ecological science. So scientists from all over North America saw that opportunity and have capitalized on it."

In five years, scientists initiated more than 360 Yellowstone fire studies. They involved 70 universities from all over North America.

Aspen, a leafy white-bark tree, has been the focus of numerous scientific studies before and after the fires.

Take a walk in Yellowstone Park and you can see more aspen seedlings than tree experts had seen anywhere before 1989. Seedlings sprouted in parts of Yellowstone where their species had never been seen until after the 1988 fire season.

Above: Steam rises above tourists in Midway Geyser Basin where a fringe of burned trees tops nearby ridges.
BOB ZELLAR

Right: Despite their criticism of fire suppression policies, area residents gave overwhelming support to the men and women battling the blazes.
JAMES WOODCOCK

When National Park Service biologist Roy Renkin first spotted aspen seedlings the year after the big fires, he was amazed. Renkin knew aspen may produce seeds every year, but seedlings of this tree were a rare sight for researchers. But he soon abandoned that notion.

"They were ubiquitous," Renkin said of the baby aspen. "You'd find them everywhere."

Of all the plants found in Yellowstone, aspen has shown the most dramatic response to fire. Renkin and Don Despain, who has studied the park's aspen for 20 years, have watched the post-fire aspen every season. They've counted many areas in which there are one to five seedlings per square meter. And in one survey, they counted 1,000 aspen seedlings per square meter, growing in a layer of ash 2 inches deep. That site was in a burned bog and near a clump of aspen trees.

Why is what was once so rare now so profuse in Yellowstone?

Despain and Renkin believe the tiny seed needs perfect conditions to survive. "The prerequisites needed to have these seedlings are bare mineral soil, sufficient moisture and no other plant competition," Renkin said.

Despain and Renkin have studied aspen seedling sites scattered through the 2.2-million-acre park. One is on Blacktail Plateau where in summertime a knee-deep tangle of fireweed, wild rose and grass thrives beneath fire-blackened trees. The biologists also have monitored test plots to gauge the fire response of aspen suckers.

The extensive fires of 1988 appear to have favored aspen in several ways, Despain said.

"We're theorizing that fire ash increased the water holding capacity of the soil." That's critical for tiny aspen seeds, which carry very little food store and first grow a tiny hairlike fringe to collect water, rather than immediately sending down a root.

"Aspen doesn't root at first, but is dependent on this little fringe of hairs," Despain said. "It depends on it for two weeks. If the soil dries out in that time, the seed dies."

Finding a place with that moisture and no other plant life is almost impossible. The aspen seed's only chance for perfect growing conditions is a disturbance, such as a fire that has cleared away other vegetation in a spot suitable for aspen.

In addition to reproducing with seeds, each aspen develops an extensive lateral root system that sends up shoots or suckers—clones that are genetically identical. The fires prompted aspen to send out lots of suckers.

"The elk ate all of the suckers that came up in 1989," Despain said. Yet those suckers grew back the next year and the next. Bison, moose, voles and grasshoppers also will browse aspen.

Aspen is an especially valuable tree for wildlife and an especially controversial species for researchers. Fall visitors admire its blaze of gold or yellow-orange on a pine green slope. But season after season, naturalists have argued about whether aspen is disappearing from the park. Some blame too many elk for eating too much aspen. Some blame climatic change. Some question whether aspen's natural role in Yellowstone is anything but what it is now: isolated stands of trees and shrubby suckers. There have been predictions also that fire will be aspen's savior.

The Yellowstone biologists don't have all the answers yet, but Renkin believes elk, climate and fire all play a role in aspen ecology.

Another Yellowstone tree species, the white bark pine, has drawn lots of attention since the fires. Post-fire researchers have been scouting for the trees and surveying pine nut production. The Gallatin National Forest has even planted white bark pine seedlings in the Cooke City and West Yellowstone areas outside the park for the long-term benefit of grizzly bears.

In the first year after the big fires, grizzlies tended to avoid severely burned areas, according to research conducted by the Interagency Grizzly Bear Study Team. But since then, the bears seem to frequent burn areas as much as unburned territory, biologist Bonnie Blanchard reported.

Yellowstone grizzly bears, listed as a threatened species in the park since 1975, lost some of their favorite food trees—white bark pine—in the fires, but

Left: A Forest Service crew drives through Cascade Meadow chasing spot fires as the Wolf Lake Fire approaches Canyon.
BOB ZELLAR

Above: A civilian Vertol helicopter was hired to help make water drops on park fires. The helicopter carries a bucket capable of dropping hundreds of gallons of water.
LARRY MAYER

Firefighter Mark
Courson gives orders to
fire crews working along
a bulldozed fire line near
Silver Gate.
JAMES WOODCOCK

five years afterward the bears didn't seem to be faring any worse because of it.

Since 1988, biologists have seen no substantial fluctuation in their annual counts of female grizzlies with cubs born that year. The 1993 count was 20 females and 41 cubs in the Yellowstone area, Blanchard reported.

The grizzlies like the white bark pine's tasty nuts. In late summer, squirrels gather the pine nuts and stash them underground. The bears then dig up the squirrels' caches and help themselves to the nuts. "The bears use them through the fall till they den," Blanchard said.

Left: A towering column of smoke looms over West Yellowstone, signaling yet another outbreak of fire near the gateway community. Smoke, fear and confusion cut deeply into the tourist trade.
LARRY MAYER

Above: With Old Faithful geyser in the background, reporters and photographers swarm around Interior Secretary Donald Hodel and other cabinet officials who were sent by President Ronald Reagan to Yellowstone on a fact-finding mission.
LARRY MAYER

About a quarter of the park's white bark pine burned in 1988, Don Despain estimated. Researchers have found baby white bark pine trees growing since then, but those seedlings won't produce pine nuts for any bears now in the park. The best pine nut trees are 100 years or older, but some trees start producing nuts around age 60, Blanchard explained.

The fires claimed few bears in 1988, according to researchers' counts. One radio-collared grizzly disappeared during the fires, and researchers don't know for sure what happened to her. Surveyors did find that six black bears died in the fires. Black bears are more numerous than grizzlies and their population isn't listed as threatened in the park or in surrounding states.

Among 396 large-animal deaths counted in the Yellowstone area's 1988 fires, most died of smoke inhalation. Nine bison died out of a park population of about 2,700.

Most of the animals lost in the fire were elk—333. The hard winter following the summer of drought and sparse forage growth took a much bigger toll on the elk population. Weakened by lack of food in their winter range, thousands perished in the snow and cold.

Yet five years after the big fires, the northern Yel-

*This crew from the
California Department of
Forestry claimed park
restrictions kept them from
putting the fires out. Fire
bosses said the restrictions
did not hamper efforts.*
LARRY MAYER

*Above: Jeff Munuey
looks over the debris
left when his buildings
were destroyed by the
Storm Creek Fire near
Cooke Pass.*
JAMES WOODCOCK

lowstone elk herd was rebounding to its prefire numbers, according to Tom Lemke, a biologist who studies animals in Yellowstone's northern range for the Montana Department of Fish, Wildlife and Parks.

Winter surveys showed 18,900 elk in 1988 before the summer of fire. The count dropped to 9,000 in the winter following the fires. By 1993, it was back to 17,800.

Biologists count elk twice a season by flying three planes simultaneously. They know that elk migrate out of Yellowstone Park by the thousands, traveling up to 70 miles one way. "It's not uncommon to see groups of 300 to 400 moving at a time," Lemke said. "It can be pretty impressive when they're strung out single file—300 of them.

"Since the fires, we generally have a larger percent of the total population coming out of the park to winter," Lemke said. "Another legacy of that is they go farther north." Yellowstone elk have been migrating earlier in the fall, going greater distances outside the park and staying out there longer. This farther place the elk have chosen in the Yellowstone River's Paradise Valley is excellent winter range.

"It certainly was that unusual year of 1988-89 that disturbed their normal migration that got them moving and in larger numbers," Lemke said. "They ate themselves out of house and home on ranges immediately north of the park boundary."

That winter more elk starved closer to Yellowstone Park. Elk that went farther north survived in greater numbers, reproduced and instilled the new migration pattern in the new calves. "We've just seen this continued pattern even when the winter is not as severe," Lemke said.

Only one of Yellowstone's large animal species seems to be negatively affected by the fires years afterward. Yellowstone's northern range is a tougher place for a moose to survive since wildfires cut down large stands of old-growth forests.

During winters before the fires of 1988 and after, Gallatin National Forest biologists studied moose in the high country range stretching from Gardiner to Cooke City for about 10 miles either side of the Yellowstone Park north boundary.

The moose study didn't show that there are definitely fewer moose, but it demonstrated that moose lost valuable habitat to fires that burned the forest canopy. Dan Tyers, Forest Service biologist and moose

project leader, said it may take a century for nature to replace what fire took away.

To find out how moose spend the winter, Tyers and researcher Sam Reid endured subzero temperatures and deep snow. "It was a project of cold toes and fingers," Tyers acknowledged. "You would have to travel to where the moose were. To track moose in upper Slough Creek, we would have to ski 25 miles to get to the moose."

What the biologists found was that moose ate more subalpine fir than anything else. And specifically, they browsed fir trees that were tall enough to stick out of the snow, but less than 5 meters (16.5 feet) tall.

Subalpine fir grows in the shade of other trees— under the forest canopy, which in the Yellowstone area, is mostly lodgepole pine.

Subalpine fir that moose need doesn't grow back quickly after the canopy is removed by fire or logging. Lodgepole seedlings first must grow tall and large enough that their branches come together in a continuous canopy over the forest floor. Then the subalpine fir must grow tall enough that its branches are above the snowpack when a hungry moose needs a winter meal. "It could be 100 years before we see the subalpine fir coming back so moose can use it," Tyers said.

For some of Yellowstone's bird species, thousands of acres of burned trees have been a bonanza. For others, the fire was no help at all.

Yellowstone biologist Terry McEneaney has spent most of seven summers flying in airplanes or hiking the back country to survey the park's birds.

The park population of osprey, a large fish-eating raptor, skyrocketed from 66 nesting pairs in 1988 to 91 pairs in 1993, according to McEneaney's surveys. Before the big fires, the osprey population was going up slowly.

Osprey nest in tree tops 50 feet or more above the ground. The snags—standing dead trees—left by the fires gave osprey many more places to nest. "How long this is going to last, I don't know," McEneaney said

---

Above: Sunrise glows
orange on Yellowstone
Lake in a vista framed by
blackened trees.
BOB ZELLAR

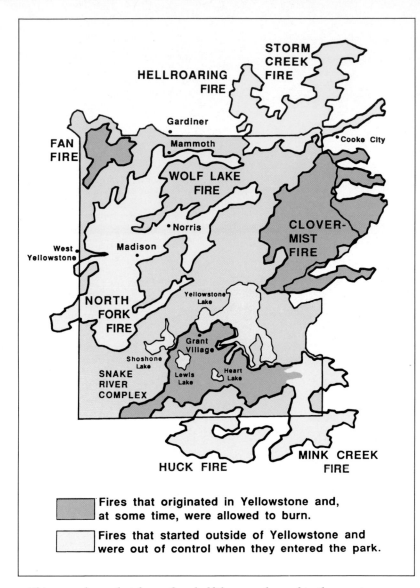

STORM
CREEK
FIRE

HELLROARING
FIRE

Gardiner

Mammoth

Cooke City

FAN
FIRE

WOLF LAKE
FIRE

Norris

CLOVER-
MIST
FIRE

West
Yellowstone

Madison

Yellowstone
Lake

NORTH
FORK
FIRE

Grant
Village

Shoshone
Lake

Lewis
Lake

Heart
Lake

SNAKE
RIVER
COMPLEX

HUCK FIRE

MINK CREEK
FIRE

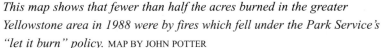

Fires that originated in Yellowstone and,
at some time, were allowed to burn.

Fires that started outside of Yellowstone and
were out of control when they entered the park.

*This map shows that fewer than half the acres burned in the greater
Yellowstone area in 1988 were by fires which fell under the Park Service's
"let it burn" policy.* MAP BY JOHN POTTER

of the osprey boom. "It's really going to depend on when the trees fall down. Some of them could stand for 25 years."

The park's bald eagle population has been growing, but the biologist believes that is a continuation of a long trend that was unaffected by the fires. Likewise, McEneaney said fire neither helped nor worsened habitat for Yellowstone's small and shrinking population of trumpeter swans.

Park bluebirds, swallows, woodpeckers and a number of other cavity nesting birds appeared to be on the rise since the fires.

McEneaney found that the relationship of some species to fire was more complex than scientists had known before 1988. The three-toed woodpecker and black-backed woodpecker, long thought to benefit from fire, thrive on beetles that inhabit burned tree bark. These bark chippers have received a relatively short-term benefit from the fires, the biologist said. They will lose their fire-provided food as bark falls off the dead trees.

Other species that are less particular about what they eat will feast for many more years in the burned forest. The northern flicker and the hairy woodpecker, for example, can feed on ants inhabiting fallen, decaying trees.

Yellowstone lakes and trout streams that feed osprey also lure thousands of anglers to their clear, cold waters every year. So news that wildfires had run beside some of the most popular rivers caused more than a ripple of concern about runoff and sediment spoiling pristine water and blue ribbon fishing.

Time and scientific research have allayed fears that

the fires might ruin Yellowstone fisheries.

"We're probably going to see some long-term benefits from the fires because a lot of the streams ran through forested areas that are now meadows," said Ron Jones of the U.S. Fish and Wildlife Service. Jones retired in 1993 after spending 17 years keeping tabs on fisheries in the park's 2,500 miles of streams and 107,000 acres of lakes. "As cold as it gets here, when you get more sunlight and more heat into the system, then it increases trout productivity and we've seen this happening because of the fires in some areas."

Research since the fires has documented a small increase—fractions of an inch—in the mean size of cutthroats, rainbow, brown and brook trout. Biologists don't say that there are more fish since the fires, but they have seen faster growth in fish spawned since 1988.

Biologists found a higher nutrient content since the fires along the Firehole, Madison, Gibbon and Lamar rivers as well as Slough Creek. Immediately after the fires, biologists noted increases in stream algae and declines in the population of stream insects, such as May flies, stone flies and caddis flies.

The insect population rebounded because it fed on plentiful algae. "You get nutrients coming out of the ash into the stream, which grows more algae in the streams, which grows more invertebrates, which actually enhances the fish populations," the biologist said.

"In an ecological setting, you tug on one little string and a whole bunch of things—even distantly—can start to wiggle," John Varley said, noting the variety of fire responses scientists have documented among Yellowstone plants and animals.

"The fire tolerance of these things is an amazing story—how each plant has its own strategy," Varley said. "The most remarkable thing to me is the resilience of this place. Nature seems to take this in stride."

Previous page: A band of elk walks through a recently-burned area along the Madison River. Fires were less damaging to elk range than the drought.
BOB ZELLAR

Above: Streams of water are sprayed on buildings in Cooke City to protect them from embers flying ahead of the rapidly approaching Storm Creek Fire.
JAMES WOODCOCK

Next page: Fires left forests littered with snags, standing dead trees firefighters called "silent killers" because they fall without warning.
JAMES WOODCOCK

LEGACY OF FIRE

Fire and weather information streams into the Mammoth Hot Springs firefighting headquarters, a long stone building that once served the U.S. Cavalry as a stable near Yellowstone Park's north entrance.

Yellowstone Fire Management Officer Phil Perkins, who had more than 15 years of firefighting experience before he battled the summer of 1988, works out of the Mammoth Fire Cache. He starts preparing for the fire season while Yellowstone is still covered with snow. Park workers monitor snowpack by measuring snow depths twice a month at points across the park. They also review National Weather Service reports.

Yellowstone fire officers have always watched the weather and tried to gauge fire danger. Since 1988, though, their efforts have increased and they have added new information sources to their firefighting arsenal.

From spring through fall, for example, the park now keeps track of how much logs weigh, one measure of fire danger that Perkins and other fire officials monitor before a fire ever starts.

Fire monitors trek into the forest weekly to weigh the test logs at 42 locations in the park. These 4-foot lengths of lodgepole pine are "thousand-hour fuels" in fire jargon. It would take 1,000 hours for them to completely dry out.

Fire officials have dried these logs by baking them in special ovens at the fire cache. They know exactly what each numbered log weighs when it has no water in it. So by weighing the logs in the forest, they can calculate precise moisture content, which will reflect the moisture content of surrounding vegetation.

Left: A stand of blackened tree trunks and new pines that sprouted since the fire overtook Old Faithful. The famous geyser's eruptions weren't interrupted by forest fire. BOB ZELLAR

OVERMATURE FOREST	FIRE	0-60 YEARS	60-150 YEARS	150-300 YEARS	300-400 YEARS

Yellowstone's lodgepole forests have a 250-to-400-year cycle, which ends with fire. After the fire, ground cover and lodgepole seedlings sprout on the forest floor, creating thousands of new trees. The lodgepoles thin themselves out over centuries, eventually yielding to spruce and fir trees. Lightning often starts fires in what is classified as an "overmature" lodgepole forest. ART BY JOHN POTTER

In early July 1988, the thousand-hour fuels were dropping to 12 percent moisture content in Yellowstone forests. By August 1988, they had a moisture content of 7 percent—the lowest ever recorded in Yellowstone.

As the thousand-hour fuels dry out, lightning strikes will start more fires, Perkins explained. "As they continue to dry further, we'll see several acre-size fires. And, when they get down below 10 percent and there's wind, we can see big fires."

Every afternoon about 1 p.m., "10-hour sticks," smaller editions of the thousand-hour logs, are weighed at 10 weather stations around the park. That information, along with weather readings, is relayed to Mammoth. Two remote weather stations transmit information by satellite.

Robert Barbee, Yellowstone Park superintendent during the fires, said he and other federal land managers learned from the fiery summer.

"I think we're in a lot better shape," Barbee said, reflecting on fire policy five years after the big fires. "I also believe in my heart of hearts nothing would have prevented 1988. The last thing we learned is nature is not a gentle hostess. We had the best firefighting technology in the United States. And those professionals that manage wildfires were all here. And we got our tail kicked all over the map. There are circumstances beyond anybody's control."

In summer 1988 and afterward, Barbee defended the park's natural fire policy.

Barbee was the focus for criticism of policies that allowed some lightning fires, such as the Clover, Mist and Shoshone fires to burn in Yellowstone and the Storm Creek Fire to burn in nearby forests for a time without being fought. After the hot summer, the U.S. Departments of Agriculture and Interior put a moratorium on all such fires. All fires everywhere on the federal lands were to be suppressed until new, improved fire management plans were adopted, covering all fires,

*Right: Indian paintbrush
adds splashes of orange-
red to Blacktail Plateau.
The meadow is covered
with green plants years
after burning in 1988.*
BOB ZELLAR

Left: An elk calf returns to the burned forest.
BOB ZELLAR

Top: Intense heat from forest fires causes lodgepole cones to pop open and release their seeds. Some of the seeds will sprout, while others provide food for squirrels and mice.
BOB ZELLAR

Bottom: A computer-generated image taken by a LANDSAT satellite in October shows the burned areas of Yellowstone in red. The image demonstrates the mosaic pattern the fires created. COURTESY USGS EROS DATA CENTER

Above: Shimmering, golden aspen shade a bull elk and two cows near Mammoth. A summer of fire and drought followed by a hard winter took a heavy toll on Yellowstone's northern elk herd. The population bounced back, returning to pre-fire size within five years. BOB ZELLAR

including what the departments call "prescribed natural fire." The term means lightning-caused fires that park and forest managers allow to burn under certain conditions.

The decision was made by two departments because Yellowstone National Park is administered by the Interior Department while the USDA has jurisdiction over national forests.

The natural fire policy first had been adopted in Yellowstone Park in 1972 as part of a philosophy of natural regulation that evolved from a 1960s study of the national parks. The Leopold Report called for managing the parks to make them appear more like they did when the first white explorers saw them. In adopting this philosophy, park managers would no longer cull herds of wildlife or feed garbage to bears. The animals would live according to natural selection and feed on natural food sources. And fires started by lightning would be allowed to play their natural role in renewing forests and clearing meadows.

There were limits to the natural fire policy: lightning fires would be fought if they threatened human life, buildings, natural features or endangered species.

Despite heat generated during the 1988 fires, the federal agencies upheld the policy of letting some lightning fires burn naturally. Five years after the Yellow-

Above: Bison calves nestle between fallen tree trunks on a sunny summer day. BOB ZELLAR

Right: Some deer, elk and moose were trapped in quickly moving firestorms and died.
JAMES WOODCOCK

Next page: A National Park Service photographer walks across a burned area near Canyon, where blown-down logs contributed to intense burning. LARRY MAYER

Above: Young lodge-poles and other green plants retake one of the hottest burn areas between Canyon and Norris. Trees had blown down here before the *North Fork Fire arrived in 1988 and turned the fallen trees to ash. This is the same area that looks so desolate immediately after the fire in the photograph on the previous two pages.* BOB ZELLAR

stone fires, new natural burn plans were in force in the national forests, wilderness areas and two national parks—Yellowstone and its southern neighbor, Grand Teton. The new policies appear to be more conservative, requiring more specific guidelines for letting lightning fires burn.

The forests and parks still have a policy of putting out all fires caused by people.

The new fire management plan for the Absaroka-Beartooth Wilderness in the Custer National Forest includes a more detailed approval process for prescribed natural fire, Fire Management Officer Larry Smith said. The Absaroka-Beartooth Wilderness spans Montana's highest mountains and fragile alpine tundra outside Yellowstone's northeast corner where the Storm Creek Fire started in July 1988.

Above: Trumpeter swans glide across the Madison River. Oblivious to all the fire activity around them, this pair stayed in the area throughout the summer. BOB ZELLAR

A more in-depth weather analysis is included, thanks to computer technology developed within five years after the Yellowstone fires, said Smith, a 27-year veteran of the Forest Service. These new computer programs are in use by government firefighting agencies nationwide.

"It should be clear that long-range forest fire predictions will always be fraught with uncertainty," Richard Rothermel, a U.S. Forest Service fire behavior expert wrote in a review of predictions made during the Yellowstone fires. "But we have learned a great deal about fire behavior and the possible range of fire weather conditions from the 1988 fire season."

Rothermel, a fire researcher working out of the Intermountain Research Station at Missoula, Montana, was part of a six-person team of fire behavior analysts called to Yellowstone from all over the country on July 29, 1988. They were asked to develop a worst-case scenario and project how large the fires in the park might become by the end of the burning season. The team had three days to complete that assignment. By mid-August, the fires exceeded the analysts' early August projections.

*Above: Wildflowers
surround a bull elk in
velvet near Madison
Junction.* BOB ZELLAR

After working in Yellowstone, Rothermel developed a method for predicting the intensity of crown fires—wildfires that consume whole forests by burning in treetops—and for predicting how fast they will spread.

In addition to better information technology, Yellowstone area officials say they have better cooperative plans than they did during the summer of fire.

Federal fire reviews of the Yellowstone experience criticized a lack of coordination between federal agencies and inconsistencies in how they handled fires.

"We've taken the recommendations of the fire review board in a positive light and not as a guilty sentence," Phil Perkins said. He and Smith of the Forest Service agreed that agencies have improved their coordination. "We did a fair job of interagency coordination before 1988. Now we're doing an excellent job," Perkins said.

The parks and forests have new agreements that clarify everyone's role in the event of a fire that crosses forest or park boundaries. With this agreement, firefighting procedures should be the same on all parts of the fire, whether on park land or national forest land.

The new Yellowstone fire plan includes immediate suppression of all fires in developed areas, such as campgrounds and villages. It tells park managers to consider allowing lightning-caused fires to burn in most of the park, subject to certain conditions, and it sets up zones in the eastern Sylvan Pass and northeastern Soda Butte Creek areas where lightning-caused fires are most likely to be suppressed, rather than allowed to burn themselves out.

Because those areas didn't burn in 1988, park officials wanted to be cautious, Perkins explained. "If we get a fire in there, it's going to be difficult to stop it. And that has a potential to burn outside our boundaries, so we're conservative in those areas."

The plan also permits park managers to start fires to clear out vegetation under certain conditions, but park officials said no such "management fires" were likely anytime soon because of the extent of fires in 1988.

Under the new plan, when a fire is first reported in the park, the district ranger, the park fire management officer, the park fire chief, chief ranger and a fire behavior analyst must quickly determine whether the fire is human-caused or lightning-caused and whether it should be suppressed.

All human-caused fires are supposed to be put out. If it's a lightning fire, the committee makes its recommendation to the park superintendent. The decision to fight or let burn is the superintendent's.

Any fire being managed as natural must be reviewed every day to see if circumstances have changed to warrant putting it out. Weather, burning conditions, the availability of firefighters and other firefighting resources—such as airplanes—are weighed in decisions on continuing natural burns.

Fires that will test the limits of the new plan have not happened yet. In 1992, the first season under the new firefighting plan, the park had 30 fires. Sixteen of 27 lightning-caused fires were declared natural fires and consumed a total of 2 acres before burning themselves out. The biggest fire of 1992 was a researcher's grass fire that got out of control and burned 480 acres of grass land.

In 1993, an unusually wet year for Yellowstone, the park had only 10 fires, including seven started by lightning. Five of the lightning fires were allowed to burn. The 1993 fires added up to a single acre burned.

By contrast, 45 fires started in the park in 1988, burning about 301,880 acres. Five large fires that started outside the park moved in and burned about 492,000 acres. It was the biggest fire season in 115 years of Yellowstone history.

At the Mammoth Fire Cache, fire equipment and people keep ready for the next fires, but they still talk about the fiery summer of 1988.

"The last really large fires were the 1910 fires," Perkins said, recalling the historic fires in the Northern Rockies. "That's what I've always heard talked about in my career. Nineteen eighty-eight is the year we'll talk about forever now."

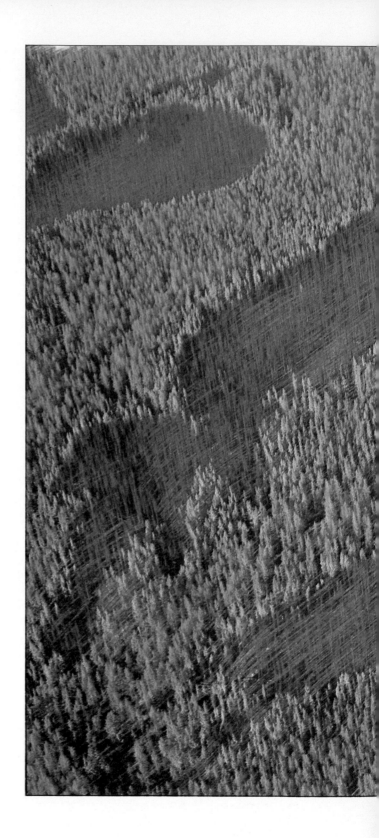

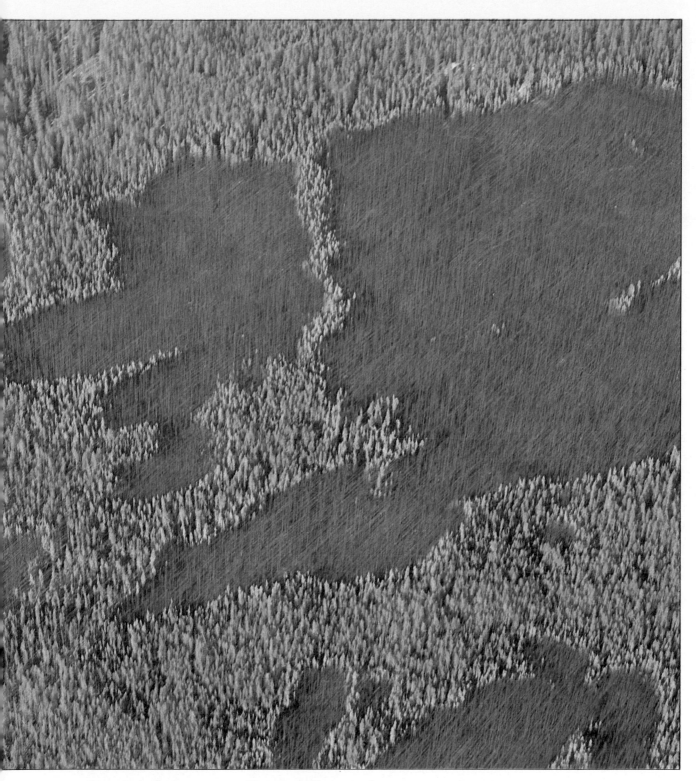

Above: Irregular burn patterns caused by spot fires leave blackened areas as varied in shape as the clouds in the sky. This aerial photo shows the spotting activity on the North Fork Fire near West Yellowstone.
LARRY MAYER

Next page: Elk cows and calves graze the lush, green grass of a summer after the fires along the Madison River.
BOB ZELLAR

ABOUT THE AUTHORS AND THE PHOTOGRAPHERS

Robert Ekey was a reporter with *The Billings Gazette* from 1984 to 1990. He is currently working for the Greater Yellowstone Coalition and lives in Bozeman, Montana.

James Woodcock was a freelance photographer before joining the staff of *The Billings Gazette* in 1985. He has a degree in communications from Eastern Montana College. His work has appeared in *Business Week, Audubon, Country* and *News Photographer*. He, his wife, Marybeth, and son, Tanner, reside in Billings.

Larry Mayer, chief photographer for *The Billings Gazette*, joined the *Gazette* staff in 1977. His work has appeared in the *New York Times, Time, Newsweek, U.S. News and World Report, American West,* Associated Press, United Press International and National Wildlife. Born in Livingston, Montana, he now lives in Billings with his wife, Joyce, and children Eric and Alec.

Judy Tell began her photojournalism career in 1977 and was on *The Billings Gazette* staff from 1985 to 1989. She is currently a photo editor in Ann Arbor, Michigan.

Bob Zellar started his career in photojournalism in Minnesota in 1976 and joined the staff of *The Billings Gazette* in 1980. He studied photojournalism at the University of Minnesota. His work has appeared in *National Geographic* magazine, *U.S. News and World Report* and the Associated Press. He and his wife, Pat, and daughter, Amanda, live in Billings.

Pat Bellinghausen, *Gazette* assistant city editor, earned a journalism degree at the University of Missouri–Columbia. She moved to Montana in 1982 to report for *The Billings Gazette.* She lives in Billings with her husband, Bob, and daughter, Amanda.